DEVOTIONS FOR
A New Mother

DEVOTIONS FOR
A New Mother

Mildred Tengbom

BETHANY HOUSE PUBLISHERS
MINNEAPOLIS, MINNESOTA 55438
A Division of Bethany Fellowship, Inc.

Photos by Dick Easterday, Fred Renich and Larry Swenson

Scripture not otherwise identified is from the King James Version of the Bible.

Scripture quotations identified LB are from The Living Bible, Copyright © 1971 by Tyndale House Publishers, Wheaton, Illinois 60187. All rights reserved.

Scripture quotations identified TEV are from Today's English Version of the New Testament, Copyright © by American Bible Society 1966, 1971.

Scripture quotations identified RSV are from the Revised Stardard Version of the Bible, copyrighted 1946, 1952 © 1971 and 1973.

Permission to quote poem "I was Called to Sing" by Kerstin Holmlund from *Lutheran Woman*, October 1975, granted by the author.

Originally published under the title, *A Life to Cherish*
by Fleming H. Revell Company

Devotions for a New Mother
Mildred Tengbom

ISBN 0-87123-294-4

Published by Bethany House Publishers
A Division of Bethany Fellowship, Inc.
6820 Auto Club Road, Minneapolis, Minnesota 55438

Printed in the United States of America

Presented to :

_____

From :

_____

Date :

_____

A Word From the Author

Environment does make a difference. The atmosphere we as parents provide can do much towards making our children become the kind of persons they will be. We hold awesome power in our hands. We actually can do much to shape our children.

All of us want socially well-adjusted, happy children who can find their niche in life and make their own unique contributions. What then can we do specifically towards accomplishing these goals?

1. We can cultivate a strong relationship of love and trust between our children and us.

This is important if our children are going to experience full social growth. Our children must know we love them. They also need to learn to respond to our love. If children do not experience love and learn to respond, in later life as adults they will only use people.

A solid relationship of love and trust is necessary for intellectual learning as well. Happy children learn easily. Unhappy children are usually full of fears and anxieties, self-doubt and low self-esteem, and all of these thwart and hinder intellectual growth and stifle curiosity and creativity.

2. We can provide a stable home atmosphere where love unites all.

This does not mean that there never will be fighting or tensions or disagreements. It does mean that children see how differences are reconciled and how peace is maintained or restored. The home can be the school where children learn the art of getting along with others.

But the children also need the security of a stable home and freedom from anxiety that mother and father will separate and one of them abandon them.

3. We can encourage our children to learn.

Children will learn only if adults will grant them freedom to satisfy their natural curiosity. Let us stimulate their quest. Encourage it. Join them in their explorations and discoveries through mobiles, pictures, books, music, rich language, questions, observations, and interaction with other people.

Devotions for a New Mother was written to reflect the kind of atmosphere in which children can flourish and grow into happy, well-adjusted, caring, and productive persons. We hope it reflects also the joy of parenthood. That joy has been ours. We wish it for you too.

Contents

DEVOTIONS FOR
A New Mother

I Walk the Beach at Twilight

I don't know why, God, but here on the beach I can think. The breakers washing in, the sea gulls dipping and flying overhead, the dark gray clouds, heavy with rain, moving up from the horizon, the wind whipping my hair, the salty mist stinging my face—all help to clear my troubled mind.

Sometimes, Father, I feel so overwhelmed. Life has become so complex. Demand after demand pushes its way into my life. I have become so many people, owing allegiance and loyalty and love to so many others that momentarily I become confused and need to turn to you for a sure word of direction again.

I am a wife, the chosen, beloved helpmeet of a wonderful man. I am also in the process of becoming a mother, a co-creator with God and my husband of an individual whose life I must mold, not only for this life, but for all eternity. The awe and wonder of it still fill my soul.

But I am also a citizen of this vast, beautiful and rich country in which I live. I am and always shall be deeply grateful for all my country has given me, but I realize also I have certain responsibilities to fulfill because of it.

Absorbed as I am in the lives of others, something deep within me never lets me forget that I am also an individual, a unique being, endowed by God with certain distinctive abilities, given to me that I might contribute in some small way to the happiness and welfare of others.

I also am—and I never cease to wonder at it—Your child, Father. I thank You that the sacrifice of Your Son made this relationship possible. This relationship brings life into focus for me, lifts me out of despair, puts courage in my heart, and gives me the faith to believe that in the end all will be well.

Here on the beach, when I tip my head and let my eyes sweep the dome above me and consider interstellar space, I want to kneel and worship. When the frothy waves wash up over my bare feet, pushing the sand between my toes, reminding me that their bounds have been set (thus far they may come, no farther), I want to fling out my arms in joy that You, God, are in control. And when I turn my back to the sea and face the city, where the evening lights are beginning to twinkle, though my heart weeps with You that so many thousands are estranged from You, yet I thank You that You are their Savior, that You love and care.

I, too, care, Father, desperately.

I want to understand what is important to my husband and help him realize his goals.

I want to be able to listen—really listen—to our children, when we get them, to understand them, to love them. Not in a selfish, grasping way, but in a way that will help them be all You want them to be.

I care for those back there in the city, Father. The smug,

self-satisfied ones who don't need You. The frustrated, angry ones. The lonely ones. Those who are constantly downgraded. The children of broken homes. The confused students in the colleges and universities. The homesick overseas students studying in our land. The forgotten old people—the undesirables! The blacks and Mexicans and Indians, and, and, and. . . .

I care, Father. I do, because You have poured into my heart Your own love and concern.

But caring is not enough. I need to hear Your voice so I can understand what You want me, as an individual, to do. I can't do it all. But with Your enabling, I can do what You ask me to do.

That's why I'm walking the beach tonight, Father.

In this busy, crowded world of ours help me to be wise. I clutch in my hands Your Word. Help me to clasp it to my heart. Instruct me through it.

Help me to be patient, to understand I can trust You to lead me step-by-step. As I act in obedience, surely You will show me what I should do next. So, Father, all I need to know now is what You want me to do first?

In the quietness of this hour, speak to me.

Then I know I shall go walking through the days ahead, confident of my calling, assured of Your leading, strong in Your provision, exulting in my privilege, and serene in my hope and expectation.

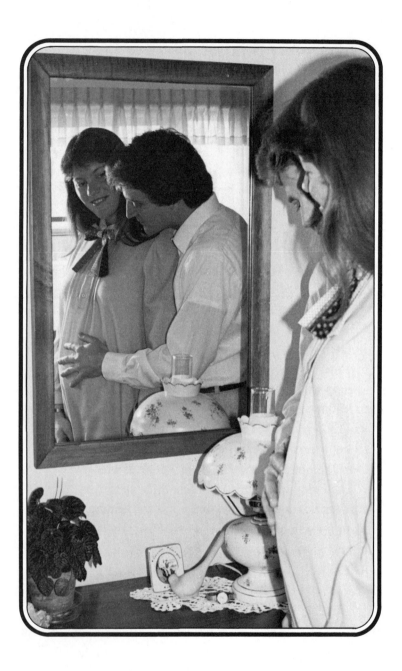

My Baby Stirred Within Me

I woke up last night when my baby stirred within me.
With awe, I lay motionless, wondering.

Then a gentle wave rippled across me again.

I laid my hand gently on my tummy and felt the flesh move under my fingers like a very quiet, full swell on a summer lake. The kind that gently rocks an anchored boat because the waters were disturbed by a motor boat that passed far off.

Somehow that moment my baby became real to me.

With my other hand I reached across and ran my fingers through my husband's hair.

"Huhhh?"

"Want to feel something?" I guided his hand to where mine was resting. We lay in the dark, not talking, waiting. After what seemed like a long while there was that same faint ripple, then a sudden movement up that collided with my husband's hand.

He chuckled.

"He'll make a good football player," he said contentedly and rolled over and went back to sleep.

I was too excited to sleep. The awe of becoming, with God and my husband, a co-creator of a human being, a being who would live forever, captivated me.

To create is one of man's basic needs.

So he busies himself with arts and crafts and skills.

He builds houses, churches, bridges, freeways.

He cooks, bakes, decorates his home.

He designs and sews, knits and crochets.

He paints and sculptures.

Composes music. Plays musical instruments. Studies voice.

But to be able to create a human being who will breathe and move, walk and talk, love and hate, feel, think, work . . . and know God! Oh, the wonder of it!

I think so much about what our child will be like. He will be part me, part my husband, part my husband's gentle, patient father, part my good-humored, sociable father, and part my industrious, courageous mother. Who knows how many other forebearers will contribute to making him a unique person?

God, thank You for allowing us mortals to share with You the joy and wonder of creation.

As my child grows, help me remember he is mine, yet not mine. He is Yours.

Enable me to give him freedom to become the distinct human being You want him to be. We have dreams for him, but may those dreams be inspired and purified by You. And if my child does not share them, give us grace to let him go his way. Never give up on him, Father. Perfect Your work in him. You are the great, the all-wise Creator.

I Wonder If John Knows How Much I Need Him

I wonder if John knows how much I need him these days.

Having a baby is a new experience for me.

What will it be like, I wonder?

Sometimes, especially at night, I get scared.

Then I wish I could reach over and awaken John and ask him to put his arms around me. I'd feel better. I wonder if John knows how much I need him.

I dared to do it. I told John how much I needed him.

Last night I awakened, scared again.

Will it hurt much, I wondered? Will I be able to bear the pain? Will the baby be alright? What if he isn't? What if he's blind? Or deaf? What if, what if. . . .

I moved closer to John to be comforted by his nearness. He awakened. Both arms encircled me tenderly.

I cried a little then and told him all my fears.

He smoothed my hair back and kissed away my tears —and fears.

"I needed you, John," I said.

"I'm glad," he said, kissing me again. "Sometimes these days I've felt so useless. It seems as though you're doing it all. I'm glad you let me know you needed me."

And then we both fell asleep.

What Will Our Baby Be Like?

My baby has become so real to me, even though I cannot see him yet. With John gone most of the day my baby is my constant companion.

I wonder so much what he'll be like! It won't be long before I'll know if he is redhead, blonde or dark-haired. What if he has freckles? Do *babies* have freckles? I've never thought about that before!

I'll know whether his eyes are blue or brown, whether his nose is a strawberry or rutabaga. He might even surprise me by being a girl!

It'll take longer for me to discover what his personality is like. Will he be cute? Extroverted? Aggressive? Or quiet, reflective, and considerate? Or maybe even downright shy and indecisive? That would be hard for John to accept.

"He's going to be a great football player," John observed last night watching my smock jump nervously.

"You're sure?" I asked. "What if he's a librarian?"

"A . . . what?" he yelled and shot out of his chair.

"A librarian," I repeated calmly. "His grandfather, after all, loves books."

John snorted and stamped out of the room.

Oh, oh! I'm afraid we could have a little problem, Lord. What if our son doesn't want to be a football player? I have a feeling John and I are going to have to talk about this again. 'Course Baby won't go into training right away, but we'd better face now what our anticipations are, see if they differ, and if so, see what we can do about it. We'll need to talk about to what extent we are going to try and guide our son too.

Thinking about all this scares me a little, God. I feel so inadequate. We'll need wisdom, Lord, and big generous hearts, and love that ever seeks the best for the one we love. Meet *our* needs, Lord, so we can meet the needs of our child.

If Two Are Not Enough, There Are Three

Trudy, my friend, has lost her baby.
I can hardly believe it.
We had talked of how much fun we'd have with babies
   only months apart.
We never even considered the possibility of one of them
   not making it.
It happens so seldom these days.
I feel shivery
   like I used to when, as a child,
   in the winter,
     I used to stay out and play in the snow too long after
      the sun had diminished and the fierce cold bit into my
      bones.
I feel numb
   as though all my limbs had gone to sleep and refused
   to function.
I feel afraid
   like I did the day our brakes burned out as we were
   going down a long, steep hill.
What if it should happen to us?

I voiced my fears to John.
He held me close to him, very tenderly, and for a long time
said nothing.
When he spoke, he asked,
"Before we married we agreed, did we not,
that even if no children blessed our union,
we still wanted to be together,
and that alone would be enough?"
My love for our little unborn one has grown so much these
months that as I faced John's question,
   I turned to him,
      wound my arms around his neck,
      buried my wet face in the hollow of his shoulder and
      sobbed,
"Hold me tight, John,
  and love me,
    and love me,
      and love me,
so I'll know again
that just being together,
the two of us sharing lives,
   growing,
   developing,
   trusting,
   expanding,
just the two of us is enough."
And John whispered into my hair,
"Maybe just the two of us *isn't* enough.
But we have God."
And my fluttering, nervous fears were stilled.

How Was It for Mary?

Last night pains stabbed me.

False labor pains, the doctor called them, when they
didn't persist.

Mixed feelings chased up and down the corridors of my
heart
when those pains began.

Excitement, like when it was my turn in the play to come
on stage.

Joy, like having Christmas finally come.

Anticipation and curiosity like being about to open the
big, mysterious parcel from Aunt Mabel.

And a little apprehension and fright like those felt when
a tornado warning is broadcast.

Is it alright that I feel a little afraid, Lord?

Wasn't Your mother a little afraid too,
when she gave birth to You?

I've often wondered how it was for Mary.

Especially that last day of the long journey to Bethlehem.

You were her first child, Lord,

so that most likely meant a longer labor period.

The last day she and Joseph probably went
from Jericho
up to Jerusalem
and then across to Bethlehem.

It's about seven or ten miles from Jerusalem to Bethlehem,
   depending on the route.
That means the pains very likely had begun
   while Mary was in Jerusalem,
   if not before.
Older cousin, Elizabeth, lived in the suburbs of Jerusalem:
Elizabeth, who knew Mary's secret,
   who loved,
   understood,
   and who also had just given birth to a child.
Strange that Mary hadn't stopped at Elizabeth's.
Did she know of the Scripture that the Messiah was to be
   born in David's city?
Was she even now beginning to understand?
Or still just wondering and pondering?
What drew her on to continue her journey when the pains
   were coming?
How was it for her on the way?
Did she crouch and cringe when the pains bit in?
Did she ride her donkey, doubling up
   and twisting her fingers in the donkey's mane
   when a sharper pain than before cut in?
Those giant rolling hills.
The winding, stony path.
And then twilight vanished
   and darkness fell.
With it did anxiety grow?
So far from home!
So far from mother!

Ahead, the shuffling Joseph, leading the donkey.
Nervous Joseph.
Frightened.
Puffing his cheeks out as though blowing steam.
What did Joseph know about delivering babies?
And then out of the darkness a shadow looms.
A monument. A huge stone monument.
The donkey stops and sniffs it.
"Rachel's tomb," Joseph says.
Oh, no, God! not tonight!
Not Rachel's tomb!
Rachel too had been on safari when her pains began.
Rachel's baby lived.
Rachel died.
Her tomb.
"Please, Joseph, let's keep going!"
Did Your mother know fear, Lord?

It's alright to feel a little fearful, isn't it? Just a little?
I keep remembering the words of the angels,
   "Be not afraid!"
I know their message is trustworthy,
even as I struggle
  with wayward feelings
   that need Your calming touch.

Learning to Relax

Tension.

I never realized before how tense I was until I began these exercises to help me relax.

I want to be able to give birth to my child more easily.

"Tense your finger, now consciously relax it," the directions read. "Let it go limp, limp, limp. Drop it. Feel your arched back soften and sink into the pad under it. Let your hunched-up shoulders drop and rest them completely on the pad. Full force."

As I go through the exercises I'm even learning to drop off to sleep for a few moments.

But it's not just a matter of learning how to relax muscles.

It's understanding what makes them tighten in the first place that's helping too.

Fear and worry string me taut.

My doctor is helping.

He has given me books that explain clearly just what will be happening in my body.

At every appointment he allows time for me to ask questions.

He has assured me there is medical help if the pain becomes more than I can bear.

I have a good doctor.

Mother has been a help too.

She's so realistic.
Doesn't deny the pain,
   but assures me that
   woman has built within her what it takes to bear pain.
In fact, she goes beyond that.
She says a certain, almost fierce, exultation and triumph
   can grow out of pain
   when you know it is productive.
So my doctor's explanations of what will happen physi-
   cally,
and my mother's reassurance that I will find emotional
   and spiritual strength,
have been setting my fears to rest.
John will be with me too,
   at least most of the time,
and there's nothing that comforts me more than having
   John with me.
Yet even with all this help,
I still do have fleeting moments of fear.
Then it is that I turn to the words of my living God:
   ". . . My grace is sufficient for you . . ." (2 Corinthians
   12:9 RSV).
   ". . . I will never fail you nor forsake you" (Hebrews 13:5
   RSV).
   "Throw all your worries on him, for he cares for you"
   (1 Peter 5:7 TEV).
   "I am leaving you with a gift—peace of mind and heart!
And the peace I give isn't fragile like the peace the world
gives. So don't be troubled or afraid" (John 14:27 LB).

"Thou wilt keep him in perfect peace, whose mind is stayed on thee: because he trusteth in thee. Trust ye in the Lord for ever: for in the Lord JEHOVAH is everlasting strength" (Isaiah 26:3,4).

"Don't worry about anything, but in all your prayers ask God for what you need, always asking him with a thankful heart. And God's peace, which is far beyond human understanding, will keep your hearts and minds safe, in Christ Jesus" (Philippians 4:6, 7 TEV).

"For I, the Lord your God, hold your right hand; it is I who say to you, 'Fear not, I will help you' " (Isaiah 41:13 RSV).

". . . Fear not, for I have redeemed you; I have called you by name, you are mine. When you pass through the waters I will be with you; and through the rivers, they shall not overwhelm you; when you walk through fire you shall not be burned, and the flame shall not consume you" (Isaiah 43:1, 2 RSV).

"He will feed his flock like a shepherd, he will gather the lambs in his arms, he will carry them in his bosom, and gently lead those that are with young" (Isaiah 40:11 RSV).

God, My Midwife

These days when I feel my belly swell and move with life,
  and my little one within kicks with reckless abandon,
I feel so close to You, God.

How often in the Bible You identify with mothers and
  describe Your own loving care and concern in mother
  language.

You are the One who finger-grabs the toddler, coaxing the
  hesitant, fearful one to walk.

You are the One who applies the Band-Aids and kisses the
  hurts away.

You are the One who gives the hungry, squalling infant
  the bottle, soothing and comforting the restless little
  one.

  (*See* Hosea 11:1–11; Isaiah 66:13.)

You describe Your own birth pangs (*See* Isaiah 42:14)

and Your faithfulness in nursing Your child. (*See* Isaiah
49:15)

Sometimes You refer to Yourself as the midwife
  who assists the laboring mother
    to bring forth her child. (See Psalms 22:9, 10; Psalms
    71:6)

I think this role means everything to me now.

Oh, God! be my tender, understanding, kind, skillful midwife when my hour comes!

Sit by my bed.

Hold my hand.

Talk soothingly, reassuringly to me as only another
   woman who has given birth can.

Impart Your courage to me.

Calm me by letting me know I'm passing through the
   various stages on schedule.

Refresh me with a cool cloth on my forehead and an ice
   cube held to my parched, cracked lips.

Grab my knees and hold them together tightly,
   if briefly I tremble with fear.

Stand beside me and extend your hands, upward-cupped,
   so I may grab your curved, stiffened fingers
   and draw strength from You to push down hard
      when the time to bear down comes.

Work with me.

Stay by me—don't leave me alone!

Pat my cheeks lovingly,

stroke my hair.

Massage my aching back with strong, competent fingers.

Coach me in my breathing,
   encouraging me to relax
   and rest between the labor periods.

Oh, God, compassionate God,

who describe Yourself in womanly terms,

how glad I am that

one such as You

will be with me!

I Was Called to Sing

I found a poem this morning, my little unborn one, that expresses how I feel as I carry you in my body and know you are growing and developing every day:

> I was called to dance,
>   I was called to sing.
> Here I start to sway,
>   here I start to swing
>   to heavenly, heavenly music.
>
> As the mountains leap
>   and the trees applaud,
> I will run and laugh,
>   I will shout and laud
>   my heavenly, heavenly Maker.
>
> I can see His step,
>   I can hear His voice.
> Earth proclaims His praise.
>   Cloud and clod rejoice
>   on this heavenly, heavenly morning.

Nothing can alarm,
  Nothing can destroy,
as I enter in
  midst His kingdom's joy
    in one heavenly, heavenly moment.

KERSTIN HOLMLUND

The greatest wonder of all came, little one, when I discovered that the poet, because of the crippling of rheumatoid arthritis, has not been able to stand for eight years!

Oh, my little unborn one! I cherish for your father, for you and for me, that courageous dancing spirit that will sing its way through life, come joy, come sorrow, come health, come disabling illness, come success, come disappointments.

That Comparison Game

I shouldn't have been upset, but I was.

The doctor had let me come home from the hospital only two days after Baby was born because Mother is here to help me. I had been home only about an hour when the doorbell rang.

Our neighbor's thirteen-year old boy was standing outside.

"Can I see your baby?"

What could I say?

"Sure, come in."

As he peered in the crib he sucked in his breath through his teeth. "Wow! sure looks funny, doesn't he? Red and wrinkled like an old man. Hey, you!" he said and thrust a grubby finger into the tiny fist of my *antiseptic* baby. "This new baby sure isn't very good-looking, is he?" he asked cheerfully, blowing his bubble gum into a huge circle.

I was choking. Now I know why thirteen-year olds are called "dumb little ninth graders".

After I closed the door on him, I turned around to see Mother looking at me.

"It's not easy to take," she said. "But I'm afraid it's only the beginning."

"Of what?"

"Of your child being evaluated. From now on he'll be compared with others. We live in a competitive world."

"What do you mean?" I didn't like what I was hearing.

"Well, from now on people will be watching, making statements and comparing. When does your baby begin to sleep through the night? When does his first tooth come in? When does he give up the bottle? When does he say his first word, sit alone, walk?" Mother sighed. "When he gets into school it'll get really bad. He'll always be compared to others. And *you'll* compare him with others too. You'll be conscious of how he acts in front of others. You'll be constantly correcting him, or trying to cover up his mistakes, or feel yourself redden and wish you hadn't ventured outside your home. . . . It's difficult to know how much to discipline and correct especially in front of others."

Mother scooped the diapers out of the washer and threw them in the dryer.

"It's hard to know how much to expect of each child," she sighed. "And it's hard for parents not to compare even their own children, one with another."

The enormity of the task ahead of me, of bringing my child unscarred through all this, frightened me.

"You compared me too—all the time—with Julie!" (I'm a middle child. Somehow my older sister had been endowed with all the gifts: pretty figure, intellect, charm, clear skin, pretty hair—at least that's the way I've felt.)

My remark sent a pained look flickering over Mother's face. I tucked my lower lip under my teeth.

"I know." Mother brushed back a stray whisp of hair. "But I've grown to appreciate you so much! Your thoughtfulness. Your concern over others. Your easygoing nature. I don't know why we parents take such a long time learning how to accept our children as they are and appreciating all their good points. Maybe because we're so slow about liking and accepting ourselves." Mother took the diapers out of the dryer and began to fold them.

"I was skinny and boney," she remembered. "Flat-footed frog, they called me at school. Your Aunt Theresa, my oldest sister, was always telling me how dumb I was. I began to believe it." She shook out a diaper. "It was your father who helped me begin to believe in myself. He's been wonderful!" A smile played around her mouth, and when she lifted her head to look at me, her blue eyes were shining.

"Attitudes have a way of being passed on from family to family, and from generation to generation," she continued. "It's both fortunate and unfortunate—depending." She gathered up the diapers, and carried them to the bedroom. When she came back she put her arms around me. I found myself relaxing and laid my head on her shoulder.

"I love you, Sue," she said simply. "I only wish I'd started enjoying you much sooner." She stroked my hair. "But maybe you can learn from my mistakes. Accept your little *old-man,* red, wrinkled baby as he is and love him for what he is. And stick out your tongue when others make remarks, comparing and evaluating him."

This last advice was so unexpected coming from Mother that I laughed.

Then she released her hold on me. "Come, come, now," she said briskly, "if I don't get on with the vacuuming, the house'll be a mess when John comes home. That would never do!"

Don't Eat Me Up!

My goodness, but you've been hungry today!

You just grabbed at me when I cuddled you close.

It hurt!

Mother's breasts are sensitive, don't you know?

You needn't gobble me up or tug so hard!

But I'm glad you're hungry.

I love your lusty yowl.

It tells me you're alive. Wondrously alive! Strong! Vigorous! Virile!

How grateful I am for this!

I remember your older brother.

He arrived two months early. Four pounds twelve ounces. Small enough to be cradled in your Dad's strong, broad hand.

But how sleepy he was, as though he resented being in this outside world, and wanted instead to curl up and sleep in the safe warm coziness of my womb.

"Feed him two ounces every three hours," the doctor ordered.

What a job.

I snapped at the bottom of his feet with my fingers.

Shook him gently. Shook him hard.

No good. His little head only drooped to the side, and off to sleep he went.

So I laid him on my lap and with my fingers manipulated his chin to get him to suck.

Sometimes it took forty-five minutes to get down those two ounces.

And then two hours and fifteen minutes later I had to start again. How wonderful after two months to have him wake up and begin to yell.

He came alive!

So tug away, little one. Gobble me up. I'm so glad you're alive!

I hope you'll have the same eager, insatiable thirst for God, my young one.

Nothing will please your dad and me more.

". . . zeal has consumed me. . . ." (Psalms 69:9), Jesus' disciples recalled those prophetic words about Him as they watched Him at work, doing what He believed His Father wanted Him to do.

How great if you exhibit the same zeal!

White hot for God!

Alive! In every fiber.

Exulting in God and in life.

Consumed with vision.

Spurred on by desire.

Loving God so passionately nothing is too great a sacrifice.

This I desire for you, my child.

For I know that he who gives himself completely and wholeheartedly to God and the world will himself be most greatly rewarded.

He will come closest to attaining full stature as a human being and in the life Christ offers. And in becoming, he will enrich others.

Our tired old world needs men who have an insatiable thirst for God.

Be one, my child. God will rejoice in your vigor even as I do now.

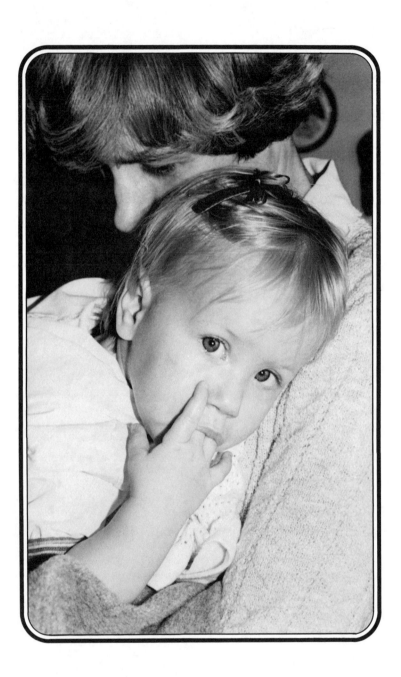

Diapering

I wonder if it would have helped if I had had younger brothers or sisters to change diapers for; wouldn't I have been better prepared for it?

The first time I gagged; really thought I wouldn't make it! Then Mother assured me the smell gets worse as the child develops—big help!

And yet, queerly enough, I feel that diapering my baby is the most meaningful way I can show my child I love him. He is totally dependent on me. The care I give brings comfort to him. If I neglected him, his little bottom would soon ache with festering sores. And the very fact that the task is unpleasant contributes to its being a ministry of love. It's my way of telling my child I love him totally—whatever.

This is the way God loves me—*totally—whatever.* How offensive I must be to Him in my selfishness, pride and stubborness. Unlovely. Unattractive. Even repulsive. But He loves me and accepts me in my totality. In my weakness. In my misery. In my dependence.

I cannot help but feel, my child, as I diaper you, that I can love you deeply during these moments only because I have been loved in my unloveliness—by God.

And, Lord Jesus, my Savior, I want to thank You for loving me totally—whatever.

Hang In There, Baby

A scrawny shrub I sometimes am, tenaciously clinging to the side of the cliff, sending my roots down deep to suck nourishment and hanging on lest I be plunged into the river below.

Strange, the first few days after you were born, my child, I felt exalted. My heart chorused praises all day long. But now suddenly, the last couple of days, I've felt so . . . deflated. Let down.

Downright discouraged and depressed.

And for no obvious reason.

"Don't worry," Mother said last night when I talked to her. "It often happens to young mothers. It hasn't a thing to do with your love for your husband or your baby. It's a hormone imbalance, a chemical upset in your body. If it persists, see your doctor. He can set it right. But it might pass quickly. Many unpleasant incidents in life don't linger too long."

Days like this will come for you too, my little one.

". . . man is born unto trouble, as the sparks fly upward (Job 5:7)" a wise old man centuries ago declared.

He was right.

We all need to recognize that a measure of trouble is the lot of every man.

I hope I can bring you up, my little one, so you are

prepared for trouble and learn to embrace it. The people of our country avoid pain and discomfort.

We protect and shield and complain about even small annoyances.

Our frustration level is so low.

And then when we don't practice in life's little surprise quizzes, we fail in the big exam.

Human emotions are so fickle. They ebb and flow. Soar and descend. Sing and droop.

How good to know we need not be dependent on how we feel.

The important thing is that I am fastened securely to someone I can trust.

My roots have gone into the Rock, Jesus.

From Him I can draw daily, hourly, sustenance for every need, no matter how much the gales blow or the storm clouds frown down from overhead.

Jesus loves me. Jesus cares for me. Jesus sustains me. He forgives, strengthens, enables, and supports. All my needs are met in Him.

So, blow winds!

Descend, dark clouds of depression.

Smother happiness for a while.

This too is part of life to be embraced, to exult in.

How else will I grow strong, tough?

How else will I be able to teach you, my little one?

For precepts will be only hollow echoes if you see me not tenaciously clinging to the Rock. Holding on. Till the storm has spent itself.

Easing Into Responsibility

Mother went home today.

"Stay a few days longer," I pleaded.

"Why should I?" she asked. "You're feeling good. Baby's healthy. John's with you. You'll do fine."

"You think so?"

"Of course."

I walked with her to the car. As she was pulling away she stopped, rolled down the window and said, "If you *really* need me, just call. I'm only an hour away, you know."

She was right in leaving me.

Bringing up this baby is our responsibility—John's and mine, not hers. And we'll manage somehow.

I'm glad over the years Mother has eased me into accepting responsibility. I don't think it came easily to her; she's such a leader and good organizer, and so efficient.

But when I was seventeen and through with high school, she let me go. The first couple of years I followed the usual path of conformity, combining college and work. But then the wanderlust bit me, and for the next two years I traversed the country: Seattle, San Francisco, Los Angeles, Detroit, New York, Philadelphia, Toronto. I joined a Christian commune. I wonder what Mother thought during all those years. But she never said a thing; only welcomed me home whenever I returned.

I grew a lot those years. I looked for bargains when I shopped and learned to do without.

Surrounded by friends who accepted me as I was and loved me, I began to like myself and to develop self-confidence.

The values I adopted then have followed me since, and I still feel good about them. Mother does too.

I learned to get along with other people—perhaps one of life's most difficult lessons.

And I learned to turn myself over to God and trust Him to lead and direct me. I wonder if this ever would have happened if Mother hadn't released me.

It all sure helped when John and I finally met and married.

We've made it through our first years of marriage.

We'll make it again now with our baby.

God, it was great having Mother here for a few days when I really needed her. Thank You for her. Thank You for her assurance that she is always on call when I need her. Help me to be a good mother, so Mother will be able to see in me her reward for all she has taught me.

Together, Yet Apart—One, Yet Two

We sit together at the close of the day,
together in our family room,
together, yet apart.
The fire crackles in the fireplace,
   the hungry tongues curling around the logs,
   little puffs of smoke spiraling upward.
Baby is asleep in the basket.
Occasionally I hear grunts and mutterings,
   snorts and stirrings.
I sit, curled up in the big chair, writing.
John, hunched up over his desk, is scratching comments
   on the term papers he's evaluating.
We sit together,
together,
yet apart,
and Contentment wraps her warm arms around us.

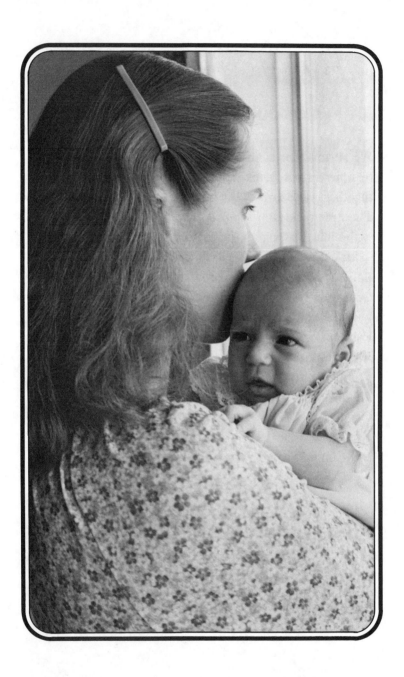

Tune Me In, Lord!

I can hardly wait for John to come home, God.
I've just about had it.
If I can't hand over Baby to someone and get away from
the screaming for a little while, *I'll* scream.
But on days like this I need special help from You,
God.
I need to be sensitive to John's needs too.
Sometimes his day's been really tough
and when he comes home
he wants only
   a welcome kiss,
   a cup of steaming hot coffee,
   (a home-baked roll is special),
   and solitude
for half an hour
to help him unwind,
   rest his frustrations
   and settle down.
I've learned if I rush in on those days
   and unload my troubles
   or just chatter about my day,
we're both soon screaming,
or pacing out our words in an even, low-pitched, frigid
tone:

"Why can't you let me alone for once?" he asks,
  he, who married me, so we could be together.
"You don't understand me! You never have!" I parry.
  I, who thought her husband would be the one who
  always understood—
    false expectations both!
So today give me extra understanding and patience, Lord.
If I've lived through the day thus far,
I can live through another hour.
And then maybe You'll answer my prayer
  and help Baby to sleep,
  or John will take over,
  or we can get someone to come in
    so I can slip out, and John too—if he wants,
    or else be free for what he's planned for tonight.
Reprieved for a few hours I'll be better able to continue
loving and caring for our fussy baby again.
Thank You, God, that there's always a way.

First Steps . . .
Toward Assuming Responsibility

You're doing great!
I glory in your progress every day, my little one.
You grasp my fingers tightly and pull yourself up to a
sitting position,
    chortling and laughing
    as though to say,
    "See what I can do!"
Soon your sturdy little legs will be supporting you.
A bit uncertainly to be sure,
but with audacious determination.
And then you'll venture forth
    laughing with glee
    as you drop my supporting fingers
    and take your first steps alone.
You'll feed yourself,
    your spoon, finding your mouth.
    Your nearly empty bowl you'll dump on
    top of your head
    while you chuckle at my tidy dismay.
You'll independently hurl your bottle across the room and
announce your freedom from it,

and scale play-pen and crib,
defying them to restrain you any longer.
Ah, yes, my child,
you gloat in all your small successes,
and so do I,
even as I pray
for wisdom
to plot your path of assuming responsibility
so you can tackle small tasks
   commensurate with your ability
   in order to know
      success upon success
      and achievement upon achievement.
You'll need this treasure trove of obstacles,
tackled and overcome, to give you
   the self-confidence,
   and courage,
   and assurance
      for more difficult tasks ahead.
The memory of achievements past
will light the flame
   of creative urge
   and enthusiasm
   to attempt e'en greater tasks.
So when failures come,
as failures surely will,
help me, O God, to perceive them lightly
   and even then positively,
      assuring my child of success sure to follow
         if we but persevere.

And conversely, make me
   generous in affirmation of strengths revealed,
   and genuine in praise and encouragement.
You're doing great, my little one.
Carry on!

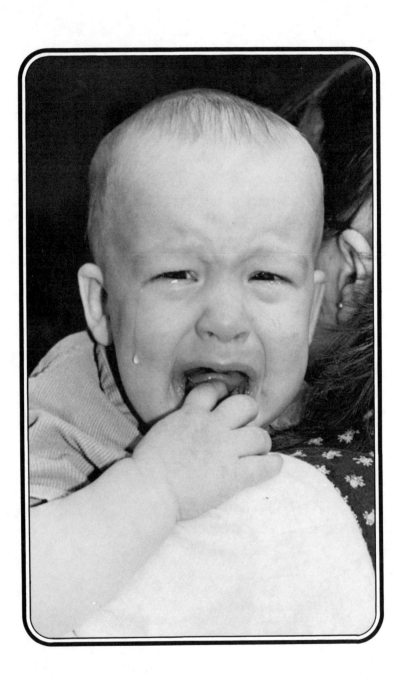

Loving With No Expectation of Return

Today has been the "givingest" day.

Baby's been teething, and oh, how fussy he's been!

I was in tears when John came home at five. He took the baby from my arms, brushed my forehead with a kiss and said, "Let's get Mrs. Olson to come in for a couple of hours. Wouldn't you like to go out for a hamburger?"

Wouldn't I? Oh, wouldn't I!

"It's not that I don't love our baby," I said later, spooning Thousand Island over my lettuce peak.

"Of course, you do." John squeezed my hand. "But caring for babies requires a lot of love. And to begin with it all flows one way, from you to them."

"Not really! Babies have their own special ways of rewarding us. By heart-entangling smiles . . . and just by being so dependent on us."

"It's still pretty one-sided," John said, shaking catsup over his burger. "Especially on days like today. I expect there will be many days like this. Days when both of us shall have to continue to love with no expectation of return."

The words sent a little chill scuttling down my arms.

"Many parents are tested when their children break away from home's restraining forces," John went on. "Some adolescents seem to feel such a strong compulsion to declare their independence, they do very foolish things."

"Like our neighbor's son, you mean," I said. "Drugs. Stealing. Running away from home. The complete package."

"Uh-huh." John was struggling with a tomato slice that was threatening to slither out of his bun.

"But can't children kill love?" I asked. "Isn't that possible?"

"If their parents' love is just human love, yes, I'm sure that's possible."

"John . . . it's scarey."

He put down his burger then, reached across and squeezed my hand again. "Without God it would be," he admitted. "But we have Him. His love goes on and on— no matter what. And He will pour His love into us and fill us to overflowing if we will only let Him."

"If we offer Him empty hearts?"

"Empty hearts and eager spirits, Sue. This love that never gives up, that loves, not because the loved one is worthy, but loves simply because the lover cannot help but love, this love is the only kind really worth giving. Only as we love our child in this way will our child learn to love. And only as he loves, will he learn to respond to people, not use them."

"The goal's so lofty!"

John chuckled. "I expect we'll never fully attain it. But we'll practice." He picked up the check. "We'll begin by going home now to our fussy baby and loving him even if we greet tomorrow morning bleary-eyed. Won't we?"

And because it was dark out there on the parking lot by our car I answered him in what I felt was the most convincing way.

In Touch and Tune With the Basics

It's cleaning day again.
As long as you sleep peacefully, my babe, I'll be able to
   whiz through my work quickly
   and soon a sparkling house will reward me.
A few months from now
you won't sleep as much,
but spend your gleeful time
leaving a trail of strewn toys behind you.
Books and magazines will be pulled from shelves in your
   search for goodness knows what.
And added to my weekly tasks of cleaning
will be hourly tasks of picking up
   and putting away.
I hope I'll be able to do it cheerfully.
I used to resent and dislike
   scrubbing the toilet bowl,
   scouring the shower,
   stooping to dust the baseboards and
   cleaning cupboards.
"Well," John used to say,
   "It's my job to clean the cars,
   sweep the garage,
   and dig the weeds,
      the everlasting, always-flourishing, indestructible
      weeds,

and repair the breakdowns.
That's routine too."
We tried exchanging jobs
   and that worked out just sort of *so-so.*
I guess 'way deep down inside
I used to dream of days to come
when our combined income
would be enough
   to pay someone
to do all these tedious, repetitive chores that sometimes irk
   me.
But then one day
we agreed that
these routine tasks are the ones
   that keep us in touch with reality,
   with the basic needs of life:
      food, clothing, shelter, transportation,
      cleanliness, health care, and comfort.
We can live without the cultural enjoyments
   and the luxuries of our affluent Western civilization,
but we cannot live without
   farmers,
      housekeepers,
      builders,
      and lovers of people.
We must always remember this.
And so now I clean my house
   with a song and a dance,
And I weed my garden without the guilty feeling that

I should be spending my time doing something more
worthwhile.
And John and I together clean the garage
and thank the Lord
for everyday
dusty, grubby, repetitive tasks
that keep us in touch with life as it really is.
This enhances our respect for those who spend all their
hours
providing these for the human race:
food, clothing, shelter, transportation,
cleanliness, health care and comfort.
My Lord,
the Lord Jesus,
spent His life that way.
I can too.
Joyfully.

I Walk the Beach in the Morning

I'm here on the beach again, Father.

Busy, busy, busy, I've been so busy!

So many yawning needs. Heartaches. Problems. Loneliness. Despair.

Crisis.

There is so much of it in the lives of other people, Lord!

People need You so badly.

It's been so rewarding, so deeply humbling to be able to minister in small ways. Thank You, Lord.

But I guess I've been so engrossed with jetting out, I've not taken time for refueling.

Snapped at my husband last night. Shook my baby when he cried and cried and wouldn't be still.

I hate myself when I act like that!

A saint abroad. A witch at home. An old hypocrite—that's me, Lord.

So here I am, on the beach again.

How could I have become so busy that I've been forgetting to come back to the Source for refreshment?

Some years ago, when I was a teenager, I underlined these words in my Bible: ". . . he [Jesus] called to him those whom he desired . . . to be with him." (Mark 3:13, 14, RSV).

To be with Him.

As a young person that really meant a lot to me.

I found so much joy in fellowship and communion with God.

Then I got married and suddenly life was like walking on a moving walk in an airway terminal. I walked—even ran, and life moved, and we just went faster and faster.

Constant motion. Busy, busy, busy.

Only crises have slowed me down. Slowed me down so I could consider You again and re-evaluate life. Painful though those times were, still they became times of refreshment, growth, and renewal.

But after the crises passed, I was off running again.

Oh, Father, keep reminding me of the daily need to come back to You who are my Source to be renewed. Daily I need to let the fresh waters flow in.

I had forgotten this, and when my family irritated me last night, Father, the waters that gushed forth from me were bitter, not sweet; stale, not fresh.

Forgive me, Father.

I've come to the beach with my baby this morning. It's quiet here. I want to get back to the Source.

Firstborn

Our firstborn.

The first to learn to walk, to talk, to love.

The first to go to school.

To graduate. To go to college. Perhaps even to marry.

A trailblazer he'll be.

Oh, God, it's so important that he be a wise child!

We hope, if it's *Your* will, Lord, to have another child. We'd really like to have four. John's future looks promising. We both love children. We should be able to provide for them and give them a good home. But today's statistics on overpopulation frighten us. How can we, in good conscience, bring more than two into this world?

"Don't worry," Mother says. "You'll find many homeless children needing your love, if you still feel you have love to spare after you've had your two." So maybe that's the way we'll go. If we do have several, it'll mean so much if this firstborn starts out in the right direction. The others are apt to follow. So, Lord, we pray especially for this, our firstborn.

Cause him to grow in grace and truth, in wisdom and in stature before God and man.

Give him a humble, teachable spirit.

A compassionate heart.

Industry and thrift.

And good old-fashioned common sense.

But season and sprinkle it with good humor and fun and love of life too, Lord. We want a child, not an old man.

He'll need patience and a forgiving spirit too, Lord, for he'll be the test cookie we bake in the oven first.

A special person, this baby, our firstborn.

Look with favor upon him, Lord, and bless him.

Space to Grow

My Boston fern needs repotting.
When I lift it, the pot is so light I know it contains mostly
roots.
I planted it in a narrow-mouthed Mexican pot
   which I shall have to break now
   to save the fern.
But I must repot it,
   or its fronds will get brown
   and the fern will shrivel and die.
It needs fresh, moist ground
and space to grow.
My Creeping Charley lost all its leaves and withered and
drooped,
until I lifted it from its confining pot
and gently transferred it to a big window box
   in a shady spot
   where it has flourished like a jungle plant.
As I watch my baby grow,
I feel strange stirrings within me,
   as though I've outgrown my pot too
   and become lighter because I'm root-bound.
I feel I need to break my pot too,
   and stretch and grow,
   developing new skills,

discovering hidden ones,
cultivating new relationships,
risking new patterns of life,
daring to question and read and examine
    what I've drawn back from before and,
gathering courage to accept and use all the strengths
and gifts God has given me.
I don't know if John understands
    that I need to break my pot
    and find fresh soil and space to grow.
I'm trying to tell him.
Help him, dear God, to understand
    how truly great my need is.

To Grumble or Rejoice

Lord, I don't want my child to have a disgruntled outlook on life.

So much discontent, boredom, and unrest run abroad.

I want my child to sparkle, to be vibrant, and to be overflowing with gratitude and appreciation. So help me to be that way, Lord.

I know happiness and enthusiasm have a way of becoming infectious—like measles.

If I can fill our home with song and laughter and joy, everybody who comes near will be cheered.

The disappointments of the day will slip away. Even fatigue will drop, like a coat that slides from the shoulders to the floor. Relationships will be tender, loving, and responsive.

Father, help me to recover the enchantment a child knows with discovery. Help me see dew shimmering on a leaf, to feel with my bare toes the dog-nose wetness of the earth, to raptly study the journeyings of ants and bugs, to be conscious of wind caressing cheek and sun, and to smell the freshness of ground wet after rain or hay newly mowed.

Set me free from nagging slavery to time so I may watch, with my child, pregnant clouds moving swiftly across the sky, and quivering moonlight on lifted waves.

Teach me to cherish all those who love me and whom I love.

There's so much nagging and snarling. Some of it spills over our back fence. I hear my neighbors snapping: "You stupid idiot! Why did you break that vase?" "Oh, quit your nagging, you dumb dope!" Or as I push my buggy up and down the supermarket aisles, I hear: "Sit down!" "Shut up!" "Quit it!." Slap. Bang. Crabby, unhappy faces. Slouched forms. Complaining lips. It's so sad, Lord. Love should be tender, responsive, sensitive.

Help me to really love to work, Lord. I want my children to love to work, not to complain about the dishes to wash, the meals to cook, the beds to make. I want them to bask in the warm feeling of having accomplished something worthwhile when the end of the day comes.

And keep me, Lord, from complaining about the world I've inherited. Goodness knows, it's really wonderful, even though there are problems. And even the problems shouldn't be insurmountable. Not with You.

Grant me a heightened awareness of life that from it may flow gratitude for all things. Let my child be a grateful child, Lord, not disgruntled. And may this spirit of gratitude abide first in me.

Ripples in the Relationship

I'm worried tonight. I had thought our baby would bring the ultimate in happiness to John and me. I had pictured us, the devoted parents, hovering over the cradle. But instead, as the days pass, more and more I find I'm the one hovering over the cradle, and when John isn't spending time on those bothersome graduate studies, he's down on the beach, sailing his dad's boat.

"Come with me," he begged today.

"And what should I do with the baby?"

"Take him along."

"To the beach? It's windy. He'll get sunburned."

John snorted. "Babies aren't that fragile! We can rent an umbrella."

I didn't go. And I had an awful day!

I didn't eat at noon. In the afternoon I made a huge ice cream sundae with gobs of thick fudge sauce cascading down the ice cream slopes. And then I finished the cashews in the can.

Baby slept all day, except for feeding time. It was just one awful, boring day! Nothing good on TV either. If John really loved me, I would think he'd spend more time with me.

I called Mother after John had left for work and told her what a horrid Sunday I'd had.

She listened and was silent.

"Well?" I said.

I could hear her draw a deep breath.

"Sue," she said, "I don't think John's neglecting you. I think you're neglecting him. Just because you enjoy being a mother so much, doesn't mean you should forget to be a wife."

"Oh, Mother!" I said and hung up.

Honestly, she just doesn't understand!

But I feel more miserable than ever.

I called Janie.

Janie's almost my best friend, and she almost always understands.

I told her all my troubles.

"Well, Sue," she said briskly, "you'd better start going with John when he asks you, or he might stop asking you."

Wow! What kind of a friend is that to talk like that! Talk about people not understanding!

What a two weeks! John and I have either quarreled or sat silently through a whole meal. We've gone to bed back to back every night. One night I found John sitting in our big closet in the dark. It almost scared my breasts dry. "What on earth are you doing here?" I demanded.

"Thinking." He sounded as miserable as I felt. I almost gave in, but then an inner voice said,

"You've nothing to apologize for," and so instead I

said, "How stupid, sitting in the dark!" and shut the door in his face.

What's happened? We used to be so much in love and so happy. . . .

I couldn't stand it any longer. I took the baby and went home last night. Mother wasn't home, but Dad was.

"I've been thinking I should move back home," I said.

"Oh?" said Dad. "Well, if you do, we'll send you right back to John. We think John's a fine young man. You must have too, or you wouldn't have married him."

We talked then and finally Dad said, "You know, Sue, in order to have a happy marriage your mother and I have discovered we both have to be good forgivers, and we both have to learn to be interested in what the other one is doing."

"Oh," I said.

Dear Lord, I need Your help more than I ever have before. I'm too proud to say, *Forgive me.* Can You overcome my pride? Can You help me tell John I'm sorry I've been so self-centered and stubborn?

I called on the Lord.

He heard and answered me.

John kissed me.

"Will you go with me next Saturday?" he asked.

I almost said, "If you'll. . . ."

But I bit my tongue in time.

"I'd love to," I said.

And somehow I feel I *will* love to.

Sometimes Loving Means Disciplining

> "You only have I known
> of all the families of the earth;
> therefore I will punish you
> for all your iniquities."
> Amos 3:2 (RSV)

These words captured my attention when I read them during my quiet time this morning.

The word *known*, my word book tells me, is the same word used in the phrase, ". . . Adam knew Eve his wife . . ."(Genesis 4:1 RSV). It describes the most intimate relationship between a man and his wife.

God's love bond with the people of Israel was that close. He cared for them that much.

You, my child, came into being at the center of the love relationship between your father and me. It was because we *knew* each other, that *you* were given life. No wonder we love you!

But the verse in Amos tells me more. "You only have I known . . . therefore I will punish you. . . ." True love carries the element of discipline.

Loving you the nine months before you were born meant discipline for me, my child. It meant eating the right foods, getting adequate rest and exercise, keeping my weight down. Caring for you since you were born has exacted further discipline—getting up at night and organizing our daily schedule around your needs. Gone is our freedom, our carefree hours.

Because he loves both of us, your father disciplines himself every morning to rise at 5:30. Even his free time, after work, bows to discipline these days. He repairs breakdowns in the house, cares for the lawn, and services the car, in order to make our lives comfortable and happy. Love and discipline are identical for your father now.

Loving you as you grow and mature will call for further discipline, discipline not only of ourselves, but discipline of you, to assist you in following the right way.

This, I suspect, will not be easy. When you stubbornly pit your will against ours, fuss and make a scene and tenaciously hold to your demands, it will be hard to hold our ground. It will be difficult to punish you when our anger has cooled. Discipline will call for enormous strength.

Prepare us for our task, Lord. In life's everydayness make us aware of every opportunity for discipline. Instead of groaning, help us to embrace the opportunity with thankfulness. For You have told us that initially all discipline seems painful rather than pleasant, but later it yields the nourishing fruit of righteousness to those who have been trained by it. This I believe.

Lord. Love, true love, carries with it the element of discipline. Help us, then, to truly love.

A Father's Delight

I love to watch my husband when he plays with our child.
The lines in his face, taut when he comes home from work,
    soften.
His eyes grow tender with love.
His face beams.
His big hands gently handle our baby. He holds our little
    one close to his own strong body.
He brushes his stubbly cheek against the downy hair of
    our baby.
Obligingly he sucks, as our babe explores Daddy's mouth
    by sticking his fingers in.
When Baby's exploratory finger finds his eyeball, he softly
chides:
    "Hey, you! That's out-of-bounds! Foul play!"
Chuckles and laughter and contented coos break forth
    from his masculine throat.
The love he exudes bathes the whole room.
I am so proud of him!
Maybe he doesn't even think about it, but his happy face
is making an impression on our baby, reassuring him that
he is loved, wanted, cherished, and enjoyed.
No greater gift can we give our child.
How glad I am that my husband knows how to express his
feelings and love!

I Had Wanted to Breast-feed My Baby

I was disappointed.

I had hoped so much to be able to breast-feed you, my little one. But you're so hungry. And my supply just isn't enough.

The disappointment was so keen it spilled over into tears in the doctor's office.

The doctor's young, and still a bit embarrassed about tears.

"Shucks," he said, "I wouldn't let it get you down. Why, eighteen years from now, when your son's playing quarterback on the football field, nobody's going to ask him when they interview him, 'Excuse me, sir, but were you breast- or bottle-fed?'"

The idea was so preposterous I burst out laughing. It surely helps to keep things in perspective.

I hope I can continue to keep things in perspective as the years pass. I can foresee what's coming:

"I wonder if Jimmy will ever be toilet trained at night?" I haven't met a grown man yet who isn't.

"I wonder if Sandy will ever give up her bottle?" Haven't

seen any adults walking around with *that* kind of bottle.

"Spilled milk again! *Will we never get beyond spilled milk?*" Probably not. But it'll happen less often. And it's only milk.

"Jimmy's got a pink slip from school! He's going to get a 'D' in shop. *Will he ever amount to anything?*" Without question. History delights to tell the stories of quite a number of distinguished people who were late bloomers. And what does Jimmy get in Math and Science?

"Tom totalled the car!"

But *he* wasn't hurt? Cars can always be replaced somehow.

"Tim's on drugs."

Trust God and seek help. Don't ever give up hope. Thousands have been helped.

Your grandmother, tells me, my little one, that as you grow, our problems will grow too in size and seriousness. But then she hastened to assure me that God is big enough for all our problems. If we will only turn to Him, He will help us.

So for now, my little one, we'll be thankful that our problems are only little problems like my not being able to breastfeed you.

Here's your bottle, you hungry little beggar. You sure love it, don't you? And I can still cuddle you and hold you close and talk and sing to you. Maybe the loving and cuddling is the most important anyway.

We have to learn to see things in perspective, you and I. And understand what is truly important. But we'll learn. We'll take it easy—a lesson at a time.

Peek-a-Boo

We play peek-a-boo, you and I. You chortle and chuckle. Your whole face breaks out into smiles, and your arms and legs and entire body quiver and respond with joy. Looking at you, happiness breaks out in me. I cover up again, stay covered longer than usual, then, "Peek-a-boo!" I cry and your whole body jumps in gleeful response.

Peek-a-boo is fun now, but do I want you to play peek-a-boo your whole life through? It all depends.

If peek-a-boo means retaining a certain quality of mystery, exposing some unknown facet of your personality or nature to your friends or mate, then let's continue playing peek-a-boo. Later in life when you find a new friend or meet your lover, you'll understand it's the joy of discovery of all the delightful qualities of that friend that's so exciting and alluring. As you search to know him and as your friend shyly reveals himself, it's sort of a *peek-a-boo* game. An authentic one that well may continue on through life. Occasionally acting in unexpected ways. Saying unexpected things. Freeing some hitherto bound part of you, giving it wing, letting it fly.

"I never knew Janie had that in her!" your friends will exclaim in delight.

But to have adequate resources to draw from to mystify and charm means continually growing ourselves. Now I watch you yawn and stretch, and I glory in your growth. I want you to continue to grow and grow—forever.

To be insatiably curious. Daring to explore. Becoming more and more a whole person. Then you'll sparkle and have facets of yourself to reveal to your friends as you play peek-a-boo. Traits they haven't seen before that will enchant and fascinate them.

But peek-a-boo in the sense of covering up—no, this we do not desire for you, my little one. Rather, we want you to grow up being free to be *you,* just *you.* Not like the other children in our family, not like your cousins, not even like other children you might hear us admire, but *you.* We want you to be the really, really *you* too, not a fake you.

Yesterday as I was feeding you, the girl next door dropped in. "I can hardly wait until June eighth when I get married so I can be myself again," she said.

Oh, my baby! I don't ever want you to pretend in that way. You'll never be happy if you do. You'll be ill at ease, tense, and worried. And this very attitude will imprison you.

So to enable the really, real you to burst its cocoon and emerge as a beautiful butterfly, Dad and I'll try our hardest to just be ourselves. We'll try to let you see our worst with our best, at the same time as you see us forgiving, loving, accepting and being reconciled over and over again.

Peek-a-boo, Honey! A harmless baby game now! A game that in your maturity can either enrich or destroy. May yours enrich only and bring joy.

Your Child Will Come to Know God Through You

"Your child will learn to know God through you," our pastor declared Sunday in his sermon.

That scared me.

I'm not good enough for my child to get a picture of God through me.

I make mistakes. I sin.

The idea bothered me so much that finally when I found myself sitting next to Pastor at the Sunday-school teachers' banquet that evening I blurted out my fears to him.

"Oh, Sue!" he said and placed his hand over mine. "I should have explained what I meant."

"You love your child and care for him tenderly. You feed him, bathe him, change his diapers, soothe him when he is upset or sick or teething. You get a baby-sitter to care for him when you're out. You'd never abandon him."

I smiled. I was beginning to understand.

"Through your love, your child will come to understand God's love for him. But also as you teach and discipline him, he will grow in his understanding of God."

"That's what I worry about," I said. "I know I'll make

mistakes. I'll scold him when he isn't guilty, or I'll be too permissive or too harsh. And I'll lose my temper—I know I will! How will he learn about God through that?"

My pastor chuckled. "When he gets older, he'll learn God works through imperfections. In fact, God has *chosen* to work through imperfections. Besides, Sue," he leaned back in his chair, "remember that while your child will come to know God through you, God isn't limited to working through you. He'll work through other people too. He'll reveal Himself to your child through his Word, both as you teach it and later as your child himself studies it. And your child will learn to know God as he experiences God in worship and prayer. In tensions and conflicts. In joys and crises. God has many ways of introducing himself to people, Sue. He doesn't expect you to do it all. Relax, Sue. Stop worrying about the mistakes you fear you'll make. Concentrate instead on showing steadfast love to your child." His eyes twinkled. "That make it easier?"

I blinked rapidly so my mascara wouldn't smear and hoped my smile wasn't too crooked.

Teething

You're having a bad time of it with your teeth, my little one, and I'll do all I can to relieve and comfort you. At the same time your discomfort reminds me that, as the ancient scholar said, ". . . man is born to trouble as the sparks fly upward" (Job 5:7 RSV).

Life has its portion of trouble, heartaches, disappointments, sorrow and loss for each one of us. It has a quotient laid up for you too. To help you accept and bear your losses will be one of the most important lessons for us to teach you.

It won't be easy. For one thing it's only natural to want to shield our loved ones from pain. To protect to a certain degree is right and even needful. Children are not adults and were never meant to carry adult-sized loads. But at the same time, they must be conditioned little by little to carry loads. If their muscles aren't tightened and strengthened and developed gradually, what will happen when all of a sudden a man-sized load is dropped like lead on their unprepared shoulders?

But how much disappointment and trouble we can put in your scales without tipping them will require heavenly wisdom indeed. Some calamities, of course, *we* can't prevent—much as we would like! But how we let you handle the daily small upsets is what's important.

Your older sister seems to understand this almost intuitively. Yesterday your two-year old brother, walking on the outside railing of the veranda, fell into the rose bushes below. He lay squalling, unable to kick out his anger because of the thorns he encountered. Your five-year old sister came out, surveyed the matter and said, "Well, pick yourself up."

So, too, my little one, I shan't run frantically every time you fall and yell. You'll have to learn to pick *yourself* up too. Later the lessons will be harder to learn. Your pet doggy will die. Your bicycle will be totalled. Ah, then, it will be hard for me to prepare you—to refrain from replacing your pet immediately—to not rush out at once to buy another bike.

Life will require that you grieve if you are going to be healed. I must permit you to grieve, to suffer loss, to know emptiness, to feel anguish. For life will present you with some irreplacable losses, when you'll have to settle for second bests. To be ready to accept these, you must indeed mourn your loss first.

Oh, Heavenly Father, just thinking of all the wisdom and strength required of me to prepare my child to accept and bear loss, drives me to *You.* I need Your help, Your whispered coachings in my ear, *Your* strong assurance to me as I watch my child suffer that in the end it will bear the worthy fruit of preparation.

No Time for a Quiet Time

Whoosh! Four whole days have whizzed by without my finding five free minutes to sit down with my Bible.

Baby's been sick. Company came. Husband down with the flu. I feel cross-eyed.

Wonder how many times I've run up and down those stairs today.

Or how many times I got up last night.

I've been too tired to read or even pray. I told the Lord about it last night as I cried a little into the kitchen sink, feeling a little sorry for myself.

"It's alright", He seemed to say. "You should know by now our relationship isn't dependent on how much you read or pray. The relationship won't change. It's just that if you can find a few moments to come before Me and to meditate on My words to you, I can refresh you and bring you new strength. In returning and rest will be your confidence."

This refreshment, this heavenly energy I need, Lord, now when my own natural physical resources have been exhausted. Quiet my heart. Relax my taut muscles—and loosen the tight pressure band around my head. Pour into me your rejuvenating powers of resurrection that I may have strength to carry on.

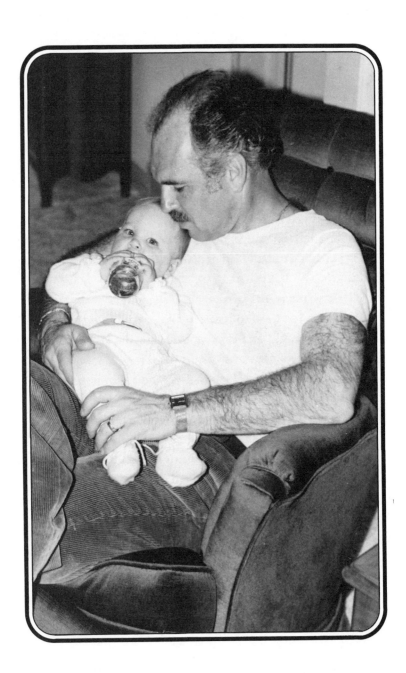

Crossing Bridges

There are many experiences awaiting us, my child.

In the years to come we'll have to learn to build bridges of understanding between us. And in crossing those bridges, we'll often grow weary and be tempted to just lie down and give up.

Especially if you become an *alive* person and question and probe.

Times change. Your Dad and I, will *try* to change with them. But it's hard to keep pace with the young. Maybe in some instances it isn't wise to even try.

When you start questioning, we'll be middle-aged people.

If you're fired with vision, if you're alive and searching, as I hope you'll be, you may feel nothing's been done.

That'll sort of be an insult to us, your parents, who will be needing to feel *our* lives have been worthwhile. That the world is a better place because *we've* been around.

You'll see only what remains to be done—I hope you do!

But we'll need bridges of understanding, my child, bridges between you and us, your Mom and Dad. And if we get weary trying to cross them and occasionally lie down, I hope you'll understand and be patient.

These are funny thoughts for me to be having as I feed you, my little loved one.

Since you were born I've been able to see more clearly the bridges my parents have tried to build to reach me.

I've remembered too, the times I stood at the other end of the bridge and yelled impatiently, "What's wrong with you?—getting so old you can't make it across?"

I feel so bad now when I remember those times! Why didn't *I* ever build a bridge? Or after my parents did, why didn't I walk across it to them?

And now I look at you, cradled in my arms, so soft and sweet and innocent and smelling so good. I wonder if some day when you hurt me, I'll be strong enough to build my bridges, and patient enough to cross over them to you.

I hope so, because I have the feeling that because Mom and Dad continued to build bridges to me during my youth, the way from now on will be easier for all of us.

Father, I'm going to need a lot of wisdom and patience and understanding in the years ahead. Teach me the lessons I need to learn little by little.

Father God, Forgive, Restrain

O merciful and forgiving Heavenly Father,
I feel awful, awful, awful.
I didn't want to hit my baby; it was just that suddenly I
    was so angry, so terribly angry.
I had never known before I could be so angry.
It was so terrible!
I won't bring you any excuses either,
    because I know
    no matter how much my baby cries and cries,
    no matter how tired I am,
    no matter how many frustrations the day has brought,
      I must never, *Never, NEVER* hit my baby, my help-
      less baby.
Thank You, God, that you stopped me.
Thank You that you gave me sense to put my baby in his
    playpen where he would be safe.
Thank You for making my legs willing to run from the
room,
    out to my bike to ride 'round and 'round the block until
      my anger was spent and I could crawl trembling back
      to the house to lie on the floor by my baby in his
      playpen and cry and cry with him.
O God, my Savior,
now that I've discovered this awful potential of hatred and
    anger within me towards this child I love,

I am frightened,
and humbly pray
that You will save me, and my child, when tempta-
  tion comes
and protect us both: my child, from harm, and me
from painful memories that will sear and haunt.
O merciful God,
this task of being a parent is so demanding!
Be my Savior
and teach me not to trust myself
but only You.

Interchange

John's dedicated to thorough research and almost, I think, inordinately insistent upon accuracy. He's been working for months on his thesis for his M.A. He writes and rewrites. Checks and double-checks. At the rate he's going our child probably will graduate from high school before John gets his degree. Oh, I know that's exaggerating, and I *am* glad he is a meticulous scholar, but it does seem as if it's taking forever.

"Sometimes you exasperate me!" I exploded yesterday. I had wanted to go out for the evening, but he was pecking out another draft of chapter three.

Usually John takes my frank eruptions in silence. Yesterday, however, he looked up from his typewriter and slammed back with, "Well, you annoy me too!"

It was so unexpected that my spontaneous reaction was to laugh. He looked at me, unbelieving, and then his grin snapped the final thread of tension between us.

How good, I thought later, that we are learning to speak openly to each other, because we are growing in our trust of each other. Oh, I know I mustn't express my annoyance every time I feel myself beginning to bristle. There's a place for self-control too, I'm sure. But once in a while it's so good to let the pressure escape, confident that a loving heart will sift through what I say, heeding what is worthwhile and quietly discarding all else. How good not to have to weigh every word or to speak cautiously so as to be assured we are saying the right thing—the right thing in the opinion of our listener, that is.

Frank exchange of ideas and opinions lie ahead for *us* too, my little child.

The differences between *us* may well be even greater than the ones between John and me.

John and I chose each other. You didn't choose us, and in one sense, we didn't choose you.

But we can come together as we learn to talk freely with one another, sharing emotions and reactions as well as ideas.

John and I'll keep practicing the art of communication. Then you, our child, will grow up in an atmosphere where sharing freely, without fear, will seem as natural as eating and sleeping.

I hope so.

Decisions

I sit and look at you and chuckle.

You're going to have to make a decision. Do you want the Cheerios or do you want to get your hand out of that plastic bottle? You'll never get your hand out as long as you grasp the Cheerios in your fist. No way! The top just isn't big enough.

Of course, if you weren't so frustrated and mad, maybe you'd listen to me. Tell you what I'll do. I'll get a jar. Look, Honey, there are Cheerios in my bottle too. But I don't grab them. I straighten my hand and slip it out. Then I tip my jar and dump out the Cheerios. Oh, you catch on fast! I hope you learn life's lessons that easily.

Times will come, my child, when you'll discover you can't have two things; you'll have to make a choice. Which do you want more? The sooner you learn this lesson the better. Of course, you'll never be through learning. I'm having to relearn it these days. I don't know why, but I'm gaining weight. So I must say no to pizzas and shakes and all kinds of other good things. "A moment on my lips; forever on my hips!" I say, and the reminder pulls back my outstretched hand. It's a lesson for life all of us have to learn, my child. Choices. Decisions. You can't have everything.

True, there's a second lesson here for you too, my child,

but that will take a little more time for you to learn as it is a more subtle lesson.

Sometimes when we abandon what we want so much we find freedom; and later, what we wanted drops out of the bottle for us too.

It was like that for me in becoming pregnant. John and I wanted so much to have a child, but try though we did, nothing happened. And then I gave up.

"Alright, Lord," I said. "I can't understand it, but if You don't want us to have children, I'll accept it."

Of course I was pretty tearful about it.

Strangely enough, it wasn't long after that that you came into being inside of me. I opened my fist and let go. I found freedom and got my heart's desire too.

You look so solemnly at me as you sit there eating your Cheerios one by one. I know you don't really understand what I'm telling you, but I'll keep on trying to explain and showing you through *my* choices, and someday you too will understand and know!

I'm Trying to Leave My Mother, Lord

I can see where it's going to be a little difficult, Lord.

My ideas and Mother's just aren't the same when it comes to raising children.

I love Mother; I don't want to hurt her. I believe she did a good job with her children. I like myself. And my brothers and sisters. But I think there is room for improvement.

I don't want to spend as much time caring for a house as Mother did. At least, I don't think I do. I don't think an untidy room will upset me.

I want to encourage my child to try difficult things, even if he messes up the house.

I—well, we differ in a number of ways, Lord.

But shouldn't I have the courage, Lord, to follow what John and I think is right? Isn't this what is meant by "leaving your Father and Mother"?

Can You help Mother understand this, Lord? Can You help her let go? And can You give to John and me the wisdom and understanding we need?

We're young, Lord. But You guide the young too, don't You?

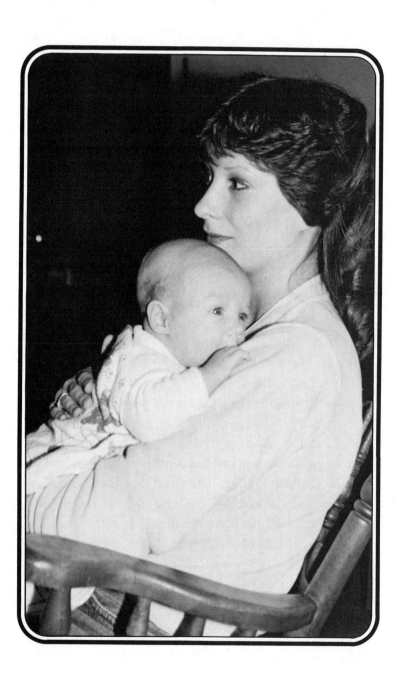

God, I Thank You for John

God, I thank You for my husband.

Last night I thought I had reached the end of my endurance.

The third night up with a fussing, ill baby gets to be just too much.

I was sitting in the rocker holding my restless, howling bundle when John creaked down the stairs.

"Can I help?" His red-rimmed eyes were slits.

"I don't think anyone can help. Go to bed. You've work tomorrow."

"Sure?"

"Sure."

He creaked up the stairs again, but when I heard our bedroom door shut, my tears began to spill.

How miserable, utterly miserable, being a mother when nothing you do can make your child happy!

I was so, so tired.

How would I ever be able to struggle through tomorrow? I wondered.

My tears fell faster than ever.

Then I heard the door open, and the stairs creak.

John again. This time with a warm robe drawn around him and feet slippered.

"I reckoned," he said, sitting down beside me, "that even if I can't help, I could just sit with you."

O treasured moment!
My tears stopped.
My fatigue was gone.
Wetly and mutely my eyes thanked him.
And half an hour later baby slept too.
Thank You, God, for John.

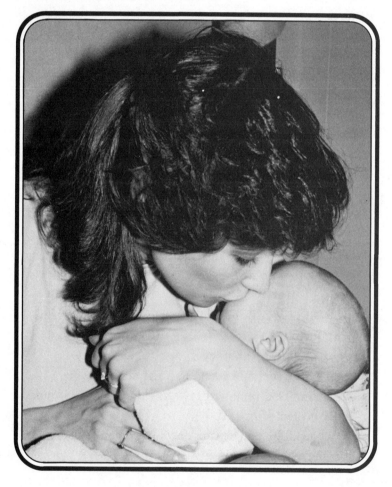

Sheer Joy

We've got a good thing going between us, you and I,
   a warm, intimate, trusting relationship,
   bequeathing joy.
   You cuddle up,
   digging your chin into the hole in my neck,
   burying your nose in my hair.
Then you raise your head,
   pull away
   and look deep into my eyes,
      your eyes alive with innocent mischief,
      your nose quivering like a chipmunk's.
You chuckle and chortle.
We drink deeply from the pools of each other's eyes.
Joy bathes me.
I clasp you, holding you close.
How much joy you bring me!
If succeeding days continue to multiply this joy, how shall
   I be able to contain it all?
We've got a good thing going between us, you and I,
   a warm, intimate, trusting relationship,
   bequeathing joy.
   Oh, Lord, let it continue to grow—and grow—and
   grow!

My Baby Was Sick

I shouldn't have worried so, but I did when our baby got sick. I was almost frantic.

What do you do when such a little thing gets sick? He can't tell you a thing. Why, if I hadn't been able to call our doctor. . . .

But we *did* have a good doctor to call, and the medicine our baby needed *was* available, and in a couple of days our baby was well again.

Now that it's all over, I'm ashamed I worried so.

Ashamed I forgot to thank God for all the help available for us.

Dear God, it was utterly silly of me to be so worried about my sick baby when the doctor assured me it wasn't anything serious.

Forgive me.

And have pity and mercy on all the mothers with sick babies who don't have skilled doctors to call or medicine to fight the infections.

Help me to remember to offer my praise and thanksgiving to You by giving that others might have the privileges and provisions which are mine.

Then I'll know You shall understand that I am truly thankful.

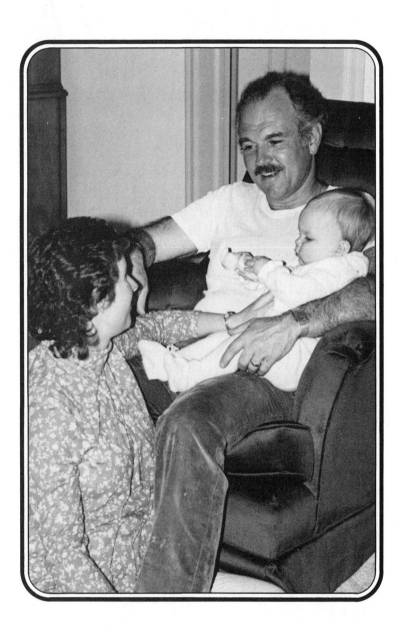

Not Really Mine

Bone of my bone
and flesh of my flesh
an extension of John and me,
that's you, my little one.
Small wonder then that I love you.
For to love you
is, in reality, to love myself.
But that's alright too
for God intended that we love ourselves.
Only I must recognize
that in this close tie
two dangers lurk inherent.
One, that even though you are part of me,
   I must learn to release you
   and know that you are not really
      mine
      or John's
      or even ours,
but you are you,
and you are God's.
Because you are you
I must understand also
that you do not feel as closely bound to me, nor ever will
as I to you.

When the cord that bound you to me was severed,
you lost your sense
of ever having been part of another body.
You feel you are only you
and that is enough.
I know this to be true
because I think of my relationship with my mother
and know that, though I love her dearly,
still I feel no dependency upon her,
nor do I want her to feel she must be anxious for me.
I am complete as I am, cut asunder from her,
and I can exist alone.
I say this, not out of arrogant pride,
but rather to ease her burden.
This too I must keep recalling, my child,
as I seek to develop your independence from me.
In a sense you are already free from me,
even though you will grow and grow in more responsible
freedom.
And as you do, I will never cease to care—
    I cannot—love cannot—
but I can learn to release and trust you to God
    who loves you dearly,
and not to worry.
At least not too much.

I Love You as You Are

Baby
  You are important to me.
  Valuable.
  Worthwhile.
You can't do a thing yet except demand attention and care
from me.
Yet I love you.
  Deeply.
  Passionately.
I love you for yourself.
  For what you are now.
  A wriggling, helpless, sometimes happy, sometimes
    cranky bundle of humanity.
Your presence fills our home with happiness.
I love you and enjoy you for what you are *now*.
  Not for what you will become.
  But for what you are *now*.
And understanding that this is the way I love you makes
  it easier for me
  to understand and believe
  that this is the way God loves me now.

Legitimate Pride

As I look at you, my baby, several months old now,
  I feel so proud.
Your sturdy little body exudes strength and health.
Your bright eyes dart here and there,
  your hands explore,
  your legs kick vigorously.
You yell lustily,
  pull hair viciously and
  smile engagingly.
I look at you and think,
  the best thing I've done so far in life
  has been to make a baby!
I'm a good mother.

Our house smells sweet and fresh.
"I'd dreaded having a baby," John confided the other
night.
  "I'd been in so many homes which reeked of diapers. I
    couldn't face the thought. I don't know how you've
    done it, but our house and baby always smell fresh."
"I'm a good mother," I said, lifting my face for a reward.

  I'm learning to trust a baby-sitter with my child once
    in a while so John and I can have time together,
    or I can have time alone.

I love my baby, but my baby's not my god—or boss.
I'm a good mother.

I'm a good mother most of all because I love and cherish.
If I had to account for all my faults,
   my head would droop,
   my song would die,
   my feet would drag.
But You, dear God, forgive me
   for Jesus' sake,
and constantly work at cleansing me.
And this, I believe my children will know and understand:
   That 'way deep down
   I do love You, God,
   and want to walk Your way.
And they will know
   my love for them too.
And this will truly help cover all my sins.
And so it is, that knowing all my failings,
I can still say and believe—
I am a good mother.

Sometimes It's Hard to Be an American

I don't expect my child will ever know hunger that is not satisfied—I pray that he will not!

But he will live in a world where this will be the lifetime experience of increasing millions.

If I had lived all my life in overfed, obese America, if I had never seen bloated bellies with umbilical hernias popping out, huge, vacant, staring eyes, or legs and arms that are but boney sticks over which parched brown skin is drawn taut, I would find it hard to believe people actually *do* die of hunger.

But I have seen the outstretched hand, the listless shuffling, the bodies curled up in fetal position on the pavement dying.

I have seen men, like animals, claw each other for a scrap of bread found in a garbage can. I have heard voices say tonelessly, "The mouse runs around in our stomach all the time," as they describe the restless shiftings and mutterings of a starved stomach.

I look at the beautiful wardrobe my baby has, God, and wonder why my child and I were born so rich.

Accident of birth.

My child and I could just as well have been born into poverty.

I am rich, Father. My child is rich.

Can You reach through the luxurious, soft, beautiful clothes that adorn our bodies and touch our hearts? Oh Christ, You who were born in poverty, will You stir our hearts with compassion?

I don't expect my child will ever know hunger that cannot be satisfied—I hope not!

But, dear God, will You instill in us the willingness to help Your impoverished children? Give us the hunger that cannot be satisfied in any other way than by doing Your will.

Have mercy on us, God!
Sometimes it's hard,
   so very hard
   to be Americans!
The burden of guilt is so great,
   so very great.

I Want My Child
to Love to Read, Lord

The joy of discovery.
Help me to enable my child to experience this again and
again.
Children are naturally curious.
    Adults stifle curiosity.
        By countless restrictions and prohibitions. Because of
        fear.
        By ignoring the child or giving meaningless answers.
Help me, Lord, to allow my child's curiosity to lead him
to the joy of discovery.
Through questionings,
    experiments,
    observations,
    and through books.
Oh, Lord, help him make the joy of discovery of books.
Many have been robbed of the adventure in reading by the
heady, gaudy appeal of TV.
May our child not be one of them.
    May he treasure the art of reading,
    value the opportunities that are his to learn to read,
    appreciate the wealth stored in libraries for him.

Oh, God, I covet for our child eagerness to learn!
Help me to set aside time to read to him:
Books that will entertain,
    delight,
    fascinate,
    arouse curiosity,
    answer questions and raise others.
Books that will cause him at the end to flip back to the front page and demand eagerly, "Read it again!"
And may I remember to include the Book that can lead him to the greatest discovery of all—God.

That Privilege and Responsibility May Walk Hand in Hand Together

John came home last night,
   slumped into a chair
   and just sat staring.
At dinner he picked at his food,
   and when baby began to cry,
   his face twisted.
   He got up,
   pushed back his chair,
     dropping his napkin to the floor,
   and headed for our room.
My stomach feels like dried-out lumpy Play-Dough when
John comes home so tired.
I wistfully wish things could be different.
I dream sometimes
   of a life
   where both of us would work half a day for a salary,
   and have half a day to share in
     supervision,
     caring for our home,
     reaching out to areas of need,
     enriching ourselves,

and developing meaningful relationships
   with each other,
   with others,
   and with God.
Sometimes I think glowingly
that if we both could have trained for the same vocation
   and shared the same job,
   we could more easily empathize
   and better understand each other.
Of course temptations to feelings of competition and envy
would arise.
We would have to rise above them.
And I suppose it really isn't very realistic for most couples
   to think in these terms,
   and maybe not even desirable.
For possessing varied skills
   and working at different vocations
could enrich our lives,
   widen our interests,
   and season our conversation.
But isn't it possible
for both of us to work for a salary,
and each of us work only half a day?
We're not greedy for money.
We don't lust for two salaries,
   or the possessions two salaries can buy.
The simple life contents us.

So if couples could divide their working hours,
and John—and other men—could be unrestricted and not
  as tired,
think what it could mean
  to wives,
  to children,
  to churches,
  to politics,
  and all the needy areas of life.
And think what it could mean to the bored, discontented,
  frustrated, vegetating wives
to be able
  to bud and bloom,
  sprout and grow,
  discover and develop,
  study and put to use
    all that lies latent within them.
Would it mean too, I wonder,
  fewer heart attacks,
  fewer ulcers,
  better all-round health and humor,
  and more fully developed relationships
    between husbands and wives,
    parents and children,
    families and the outside world,
    and people and God?

Wistfully I think all this and wonder if the day will come.
If not for us, perhaps, our child, it will come for you.

Please, God.

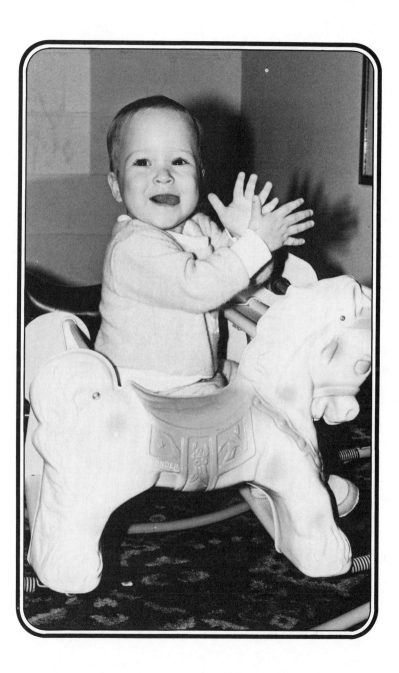